Planet Granite

Ruth Clarke

OXFORD
UNIVERSITY PRESS

OXFORD
UNIVERSITY PRESS

Great Clarendon Street, Oxford OX2 6DP

Oxford University Press is a department of the University of Oxford.
It furthers the University's objective of excellence in research, scholarship,
and education by publishing worldwide in

Oxford   New York

Auckland   Cape Town   Dar es Salaam   Hong Kong   Karachi
Kuala Lumpur   Madrid   Melbourne   Mexico City   Nairobi
New Delhi   Shanghai   Taipei   Toronto

With offices in

Argentina   Austria   Brazil   Chile   Czech Republic   France   Greece
Guatemala   Hungary   Italy   Japan   Poland   Portugal   Singapore
South Korea   Switzerland   Thailand   Turkey   Ukraine   Vietnam

Oxford is a registered trade mark of Oxford University Press
in the UK and in certain other countries

British Library Cataloguing in Publication Data

Data available

ISBN-13: 978-0-19-917952-7
ISBN-10: 0-19-917952-2

1 3 5 7 9 10 8 6 4 2

Printed in China by Imago

Acknowledgements

The publisher would like to thank the following for permission to reproduce
photographs: **p1** Corel/OUP, **p4** Gerald Cullifords Ltd., **p9**br Alamy/Cubo Images, **p10**l
Alamy/Christa Kniff, **p11**c Alamy/Brian Harris, b Pictures of Britain/Adam Swain, **p13** Sipa/Rex
Features, **p14** Jo Giordano/Rex Features, **p15** Corbis/David Lees, **p16** Alamy/David R Farzier;
Photolibrary Inc, **p18** Alamy/Andre Jenny, **p20**t Alamy/Peter Titmuss, **p23**t Rex Features, **p28**
Anand Razdan Photography/Photographers Direct

All other photos by Patrick Eden Photography/OUP

Cover phography by: Corel/OUP, Classet/OUP

Illustrations by: **p17**, **p23**bl, **p28**t Barking Dog Art, **p9**t, **p12** Martin Cottam, **p7**, **p11**, **p20/21**
Mark Duffin, **p4**, **p6**, **p8**, **p10**, **p13**, **p16**, **p18**, **p20**tl, **p22**, **p24**, **p25**, **p28**, **p29**, **p30** Clive Goodyer

Design by John Walker

Every effort has been made to contact copyright holders of material reproduced in this book. If notified,
the publishers will be pleased to rectify any errors or omissions at the earliest opportunity

Contents

At the workshop

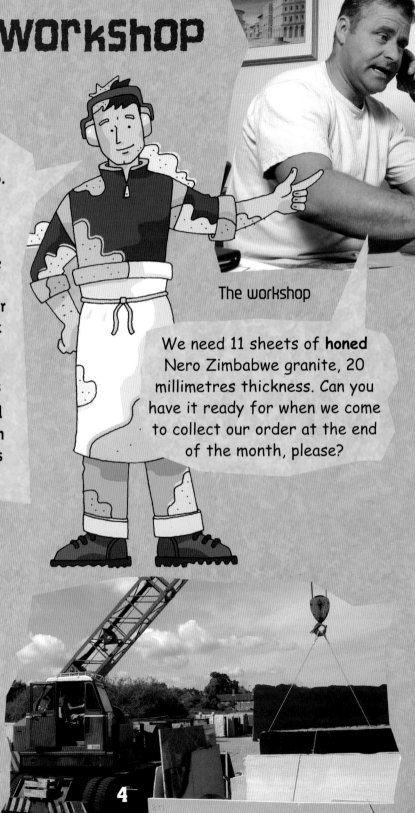

Hi, my name is Richard and I own this workshop. We make all sorts of different things out of granite and marble. I love working with these materials. They are so different from each other and so beautiful to look at. It's not just me who thinks that. All over the world, for thousands of years, people have used granite and marble both to create their buildings and to decorate them.

The workshop

We need 11 sheets of **honed** Nero Zimbabwe granite, 20 millimetres thickness. Can you have it ready for when we come to collect our order at the end of the month, please?

The wholesaler's yard

Granite and marble come from quarries all over the world. Each type may have different names in different countries. I have to learn all the different names. This is Nero Africa, but it's also known as Bon Accord, and it can also go by the name of Nero Impala.

Nero Africa

Granite is the second hardest natural substance. Only diamonds are harder. Some granites are harder than others. This is Marinace. It's so tough it takes me twice as long as most granites to cut through it with the power saw.

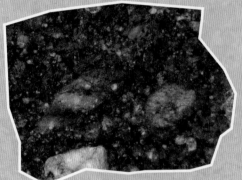

Marinace

Granite is an **igneous** rock. It is hard and coarse-grained. It contains minerals which lock together in the stone rather like a jigsaw puzzle. This is why granite is so tough and strong.

MARBLE

Some of the marbles though are very fragile. This is Rosso Verona, which is so soft I can break a piece in my hand like I would a biscuit.

Rosso Verona

Marble is a **metamorphic** rock, which means it has changed, or metamorphosed, from another type of rock (limestone) into marble. Heat and pressure in the earth's crust force the limestone to change in texture and composition. This process is called recrystallization.

How do we use these stones?

I work with polished sheets of granite and marble. These are the best grade of stone that come out of the quarries. The sheets are cut into **bespoke**, or made-to-measure, items. Stone is used in many different ways and in places that might surprise you.

Low grade waste stone from the granite quarries is ground up and used in making roads.

Waste marble can be ground into a dust and used to make special effects in sheets of paper.

Fine grains of marble are often used as the binding agent in soap.

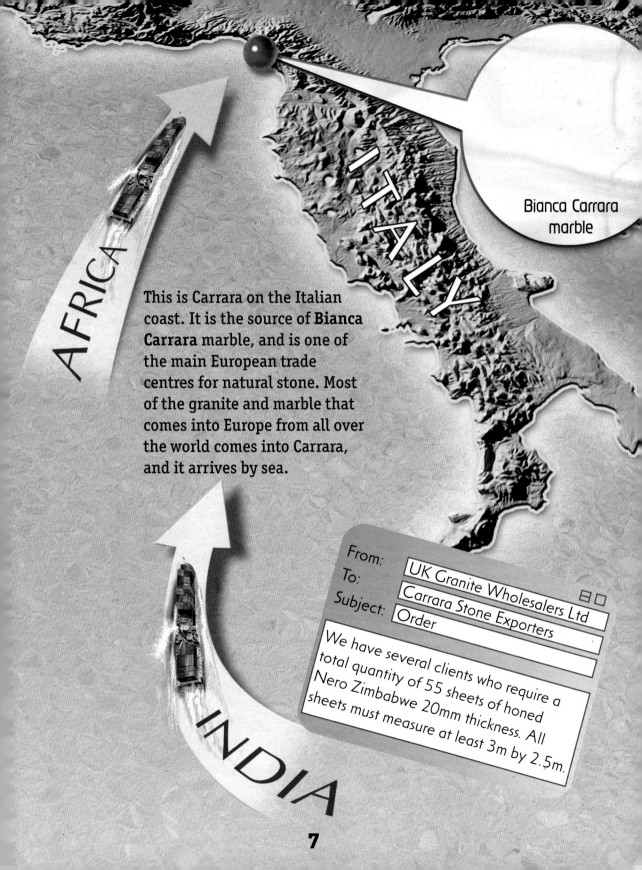

ITALY

AFRICA

INDIA

Bianca Carrara marble

This is Carrara on the Italian coast. It is the source of **Bianca Carrara** marble, and is one of the main European trade centres for natural stone. Most of the granite and marble that comes into Europe from all over the world comes into Carrara, and it arrives by sea.

From: UK Granite Wholesalers Ltd
To: Carrara Stone Exporters
Subject: Order

We have several clients who require a total quantity of 55 sheets of honed Nero Zimbabwe 20mm thickness. All sheets must measure at least 3m by 2.5m.

Making a statement

Today, granite and marble are used for many different things. They are seen as a display of wealth and success. It's always been like that. For thousands of years, using granite and marble to embellish a home or public building has been one of the strongest statements of wealth. Marble has always been as desirable as gold or diamonds.

Name: Emperor Nero Claudius Drusus Germanicus

Reign: AD 54–AD 68

Famous for: fiddling while Rome burned. Ever heard that phrase? The Romans didn't play fiddles, but Nero certainly had a reputation for strange and often wild behaviour.

What's in a name?

The names given to the different granites and marble try to capture the beauty of the material.

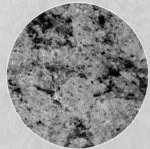

Venetian Gold — a granite from Brazil

Nero's house of gold

In AD 64 a great fire raged for nine days through Rome and destroyed huge swathes of the city, including the Emperor's palace. After the fire Emperor Nero decided to build the most magnificent house the world had ever seen. It was called *Domus Aurea* (the House of Gold). It covered the entire centre of the city. Inside, the walls were clad with gold and precious marble of every colour. The polished marble walls (which have now disintegrated) reflected the light that bounced off the vast lakes outside.

But Nero's palace lasted no longer than its owner. His successors wanted to rid themselves of his unpopular image and destroyed most of the buildings.

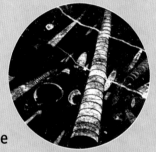

Nero Cosmo — a marble from Morocco containing fossils

Star Galaxy — a granite from South Africa

Down to Earth

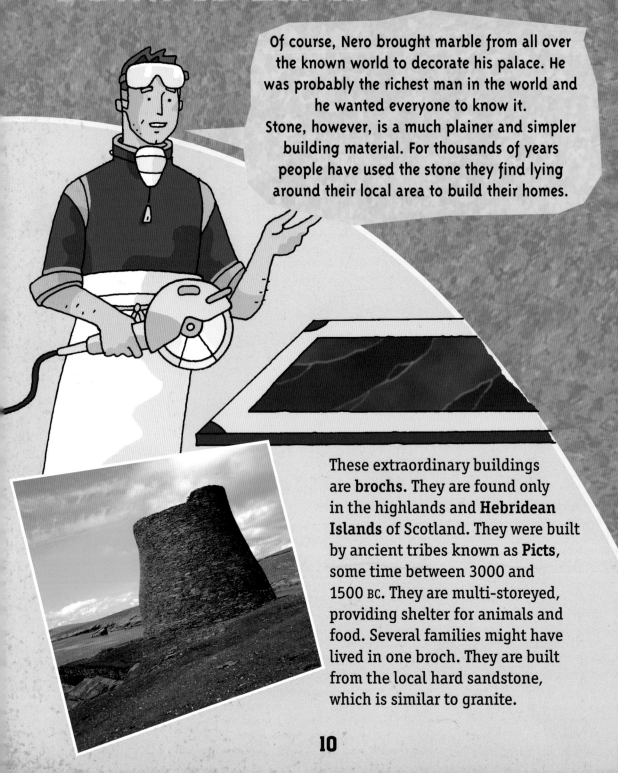

Of course, Nero brought marble from all over the known world to decorate his palace. He was probably the richest man in the world and he wanted everyone to know it.

Stone, however, is a much plainer and simpler building material. For thousands of years people have used the stone they find lying around their local area to build their homes.

These extraordinary buildings are **brochs**. They are found only in the highlands and **Hebridean Islands** of Scotland. They were built by ancient tribes known as **Picts**, some time between 3000 and 1500 BC. They are multi-storeyed, providing shelter for animals and food. Several families might have lived in one broch. They are built from the local hard sandstone, which is similar to granite.

One of the main areas where granite is found in the United Kingdom is Devon, particularly Dartmoor. Whole communities on Dartmoor are built from granite. The buildings themselves are often beautiful but the stone they are built from **emanates** a potentially dangerous gas – radon.

What's radon?

Radon is a naturally occurring gas which comes from rocks, soil and underground water sources. The Earth's crust is made up of many different types of stone, like limestone or sandstone, for example. Radon emanates out of the ground and through these rocks all over the planet. But levels are higher in regions comprising mainly granite. Radon gives off radiation, which can cause cancer. Radon is the second leading cause of lung cancer in the world.

United Kingdom

Dartmoor

Dartmoor prison was originally built right in the middle of the treacherous moor for French prisoners during the **Napoleonic Wars**. Built entirely of the local granite, it's a grim fortress.

Marble: a Renaissance favourite

White Italian marble was the main material used by sculptors in the **Renaissance**. Michelangelo is considered to be one of the greatest sculptors the world has ever known. In his day, he was known as the 'divine artist'; maybe because he believed in God, or because he made beautiful things; maybe both.

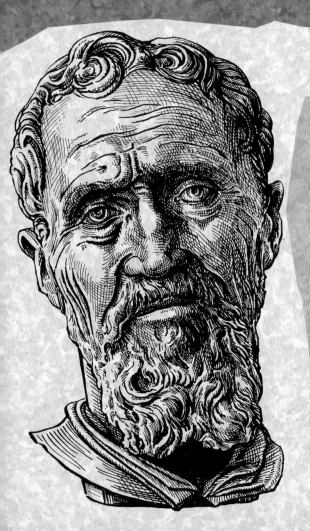

Name: Michelangelo Buonarotti

Born: 6 March 1475

Died: 18 February 1564

Where he lived: he was born in a tiny village in Tuscany and worked for most of his life in Rome.

Little-known fact: Michelangelo didn't believe he was a great artist. He thought God had created the masterpieces inside the stone and all he did was release them with his chisel.

This is my favourite work of art. Marble is relatively soft so it can be worked very precisely with a chisel. It was the perfect material for the Renaissance sculptor because they were interested in creating the human form as realistically as possible. That doesn't mean this was easy. Just look at Michelangelo's work. Look at the folds in the cloth and the humanity of their faces. Can you believe this is stone?

Michelangelo's Pieta, 1499

"It is certainly a miracle that a formless block of stone could ever have been reduced to a perfection that nature is scarcely able to create in the flesh."
Giorgio Vasari, 1550

Quarrying Michelangelo's marble

Michelangelo bought most of the marble blocks for his sculptures from just one quarry. It is very close to where he lived. Today, the marble is called Calacatta Michelangelo. The quarry is still working today and producing blocks of marble identical to those that Michelangelo bought and made into his masterpieces. Only the technology has changed. Marble is now quarried with powerful cutting machinery rather than by hand.

Marble does not split easily into equally-sized pieces and must be cut carefully from the earth. It's quite common to use explosives in stone quarrying, but if you do this with marble, it's very likely to shatter. The blocks are quarried using channel cutters instead.

I made this sink out of a solid block of this white marble. It's for a client's bathroom. It's odd to think it's from the same type of stone that Michelangelo carved this beautiful sculpture.

Michelangelo's David, 1501

15

The links in the chain

From: Carrara Stone Exporters
To: UK Granite Wholesalers Ltd
Subject: Order

Your order of 55 sheets of Nero Zimbabwe 20mm thickness is ready for shipment. Please contact your shipping agents to arrange collection from our yard.

It's a long trade route from the quarry to me. This granite is passing through a lot of hands before it gets into mine.

Italian wholesaler cuts each of the blocks of stone into approximately 40 sheets (see page 23)

UK wholesaler orders 55 sheets from Italy

Ten blocks of granite weighing 15 to 20 tonnes each mined in South Africa and transported to Italy

UK retailer (that's me) orders from wholesaler 11 sheets of black granite

Retailer sells to UK customer

The granite quarry in South Africa producing the stone in blocks. They cut them out of the rock in cuboid shapes.

Other stones

Other stones are used as building materials too and they are very different from granite. Here are just a few of them.

LIMESTONE

Usually formed on the bottom of lakes and oceans from the layers of shells and bones that settle on the bed. It's soft and crumbles easily.

SLATE

A fine grained rock that can be easily split into thin sheets, like roof tiles. It's a metamorphic rock like marble but it is formed deep under the Earth's crust when heat and pressure are put on **shale**.

TRAVERTINE

It's a cousin of marble. It is formed out of limestone like its more famous relative but it is even more **porous**. It's actually got holes in it.

A gift from nature or costing the Earth?

Stone is a natural product, so the colour of one batch of blocks will vary from another. They are not like tins of paint. You can never guarantee the colour or the pattern in the stone.

This is a working quarry in Carrara, Italy. Once the stone comes out of the earth, it cannot go back. Stone is a non-renewable resource, just like coal and oil. We have a vast supply, as it makes up most of the land mass of our planet, but what impact is this industry having on our environment?

Stone at what price?

✔ Natural stone is a **durable** substance so it lasts a long time and will not need replacing as frequently as other building materials, if at all.

✔ Every product from the quarrying process is used. High grade stone is used for decorative products and low grade is used for the base of roads.

✔ No dangerous or toxic substances are used in the production of stone, unlike in the production of other building materials.

✔ Quarries are refilled, once finished, and can return to another use.

✘ Stone is a non-renewable resource. It cannot be returned to the earth and it cannot **regenerate** itself.

✘ The quarries destroy the Earth's natural landscape.

✘ Transporting granite and marble by land and sea all around the world contributes to the global pollution problem.

✘ Vast quantities of water are used in the quarrying and processing of stone.

Can you think of any more arguments in this debate? They could be either for or against. Is the marble and granite industry a good or a bad thing for our planet?

A World of Stone

Every day of the week quarries all over the world are **excavating** marble and granite. Every one of the five continents is predominantly made up of granite. They all contain marble as well. There are hundreds of different kinds of granite and marble.

The blocks of stone travel by sea to distribution yards where they are cut into sheets.

Verde Bahia is a dark green granite from Brazil.

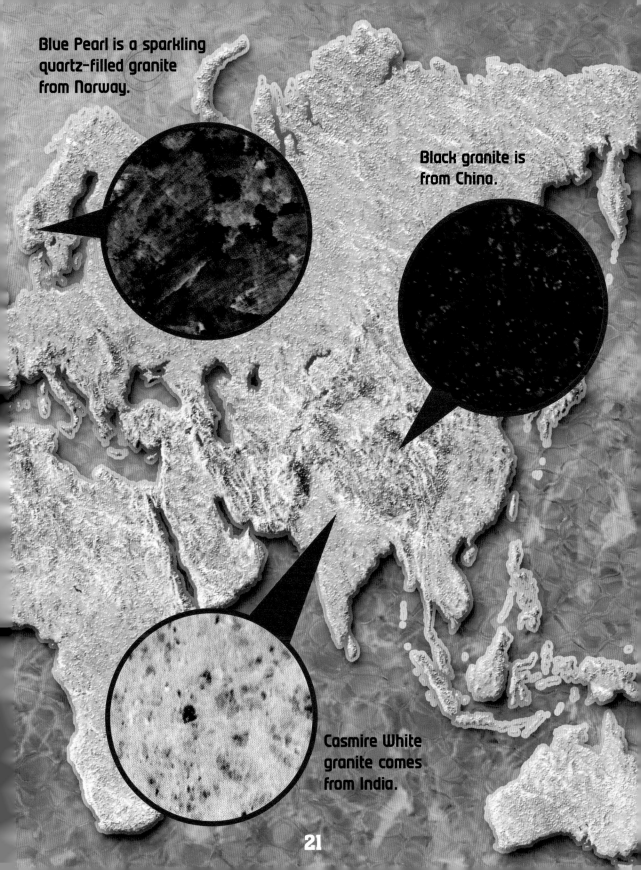

Processing and distributing

The shipments of stone blocks arrive in big distribution yards, like this one in Carrara. These yards are the size of football pitches. Some firms may have ten distribution yards like this all joined together. They hold tens of thousands of tonnes of stone and hundreds of different types. My order of 11 sheets of granite seems small in a yard like this.

Granite has a grain to it, just like wood does. The grain creates the pattern in the sheets of stone. If the block is cut from left to right it will create one pattern, if it is cut from back to front, it will create another.

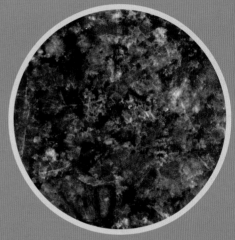

This is Verde Fontaine. It is cut across the grain and its patterning is in dense splodges of colour.

Once the blocks are at the yard, they are sliced with a special cutting machine into sheets. Remember, around 40 sheets come out of one block. They are normally 20 or 30 millimetres thick. There are very powerful saw blades about 2 metres in diameter that slice through the rock as if it were a loaf of bread.
Once the sheets are cut, they are polished on one side, ready for distribution.

Look at this Verde Lavras. It is actually the same stone, but the block has been cut in the other direction, creating different patterns of colour.

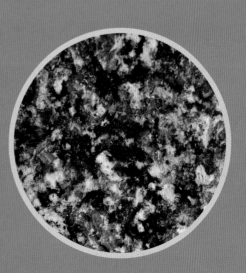

Delivery day

My sheets of granite have travelled from Italy and have finally arrived in my workshops. I have a crane to help us lift them off the delivery truck and stack them in the right place ready to be cut. Other workshops may use forklift trucks to help them.

You can see just how heavy and difficult these sheets are to **manoeuvre**. We have to be very careful to keep everyone who works here as safe as possible. Every day, people do all sorts of different jobs where one little mistake, made by either them or someone else, could lead to a serious injury or even death.

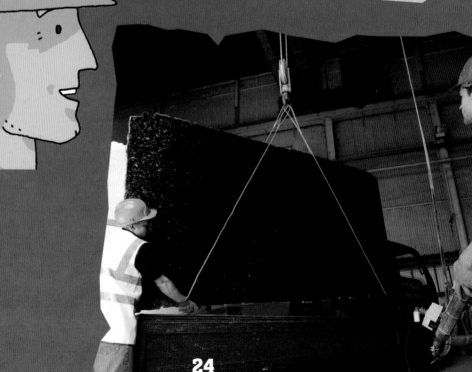

Staying safe

hard hat: worn whenever the crane is in operation

ear defenders: worn when operating any noisy machinery

mask: worn when polishing the stone to reduce the inhalation of the dust, which could be damaging to the lungs

eye protection: worn when operating any machinery for cutting or polishing the stone

reflective jacket: worn whenever the crane or any other moving machinery is in operation

steel-toed boots: the only footwear allowed in the workshops

Now we have to cut the sheets of black granite into large tiles for an office-block floor. The plans are drawn up on a special architectural drawing program. I drew this plan after taking measurements myself on the site. I can now read the plan and find out what size each tile needs to be to get a perfect fit.

Making up the order

We use a power saw with a special blade to cut the stone. As the saw moves through the granite, it gets extremely hot. There is also a huge amount of dense dust. The saw bench is flooded with water during cutting to lubricate the blade and control the dust.

Parts of the cut pieces have to be polished. This is time-consuming and repetitive work. It's just like sanding a piece of wood until it's smooth to the touch.

Black granite is the hardest of all the granites and granite is the second hardest natural substance. The only harder natural substance is diamond. Therefore, the only thing that polishes granite is diamonds. So we use fittings on our polishing tools encrusted with lots of tiny diamonds.

Laying the floor

180cm

360cm

Here is a basic plan of the floor we are making the granite tiles for. I have included the length and width of the entire floor area.

The cut and polished tiles have been laid and the floor is finished. This black granite is a long way from where it came from – the mountains of South Africa. It will withstand the pounding of thousands of feet for many years to come. Now, I'm tired, but I have to go back to the workshops to start work on my next order.

QUIZ

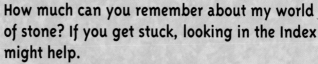

How much can you remember about my world of stone? If you get stuck, looking in the Index might help.

1 Can you name a particularly fragile marble?

2 How many days did the fire that destroyed Nero's House of Gold last for?

3 What was the name of the ancient people who built the Brochs in Scotland?

4 Can you name the natural gas that comes out of the earth's rocks, soil and water and causes cancer?

5 What is the name given to the marble that Michelangelo Buonarotti used for his sculptures?

6 Can you name one other type of stone, apart from granite and marble, which is used as a building material?

7 Can you name the blue granite which comes from Norway?

8 What is the only natural substance harder than black granite?

See answers below.

Answers
1 Rosso Verona
2 Nine
3 Picts
4 radon
5 Calacatta Michelangelo
6 limestone, slate or travertine would all be right answers
7 Blue Pearl
8 Diamonds

Glossary

bespoke – goods which have been specially ordered and made to match the individual customer's needs

Bianca Carrara – a white marble with a grey fleck marking in it, from Carrara in Italy. 'Bianca' means 'white' in Italian

brochs – prehistoric round, stone homes built in the highlands and islands of Scotland

durable – a material is described as durable if it can last a long time or permanently

emanates – a way of describing liquid or gas flowing out from a source

excavating – digging out an area of the earth by any means to create a hollow

grain – the arrangement of fibres in a material, like wood or granite, which gives it a pattern and individual marking

Hebridean Islands – islands at the far northern extreme of the British Isles, off the north-west coast of Scotland

honed – a finish to stone which gives it a dull, matt appearance

igneous – a type of rock which is formed by volcanic activity in the Earth's crust

lubricate – making something slippery or smooth by putting liquid of any type, e.g. water or oil, on its surface

manoeuvre – carrying out a series of carefully planned moves to get an object from one place to another

metamorphic – a type of rock which has changed in its make-up after enduring heat or pressure

Napoleonic Wars – a series of wars fought in Europe in the late 18th century between Napoleon, the Emperor of France, and other European empires

Picts – a prehistoric people who lived in northern Britain. Little is known about them but they are thought to have worn elaborate body paint. Their name is from a Latin word meaning 'painted' or 'tattooed'

porous – allows water to soak through

quarry – an open pit from which stone is taken out of the ground

regenerate – the ability of a material to recreate itself

Renaissance – a period of time which began in the 14th century in Europe and lasted approximately 200 years. During this time Art modelled itself on the styles and tastes of the Ancient Romans and Greeks. The word Renaissance is based on the French word meaning 'rebirth'

retailer – a business which sells goods which have come from the wholesalers straight on to the public

shale – a fragile type of rock which lies in a thin layer, often against coal, in the earth's crust

wholesaler – a business which sells goods in large quantities to other businesses. Those businesses, the retailers, use the goods to make their product or sell them straight on in smaller quantities to the public

Index